KENT PRI

by

DULCIE LEWIS

Dulcie Lewis
10.10.96.

COUNTRYSIDE BOOKS

NEWBURY · BERKSHIRE

First published 1996
© Dulcie Lewis 1996

COUNTRYSIDE BOOKS
3 Catherine Road
Newbury, Berkshire

ISBN 1 85306 419 X

Produced through MRM Associates Ltd., Reading
Printed by Woolnough Bookbinding Ltd., Irthlingborough

CONTENTS

FOREWORD

When word got out that I was researching a book on Kent privies, I was invited to talk on BBC Radio Kent to the presenter of an afternoon show, Mr Pat Marsh. Half an hour sped by in his genial company while we discussed two-holers, bucket-and-chuckit and which newspapers gave the softest, most efficient wipe. At the end of his afternoon show Mr Marsh informed his listeners that I was a nice lady writing on a strange subject.

It has been a common reaction as I telephoned, wrote and visited my way round Kent. Even I wondered what I was doing, examining yet another dank privy hole and discussing with complete strangers their most intimate moments. Why did I want to probe the mystery of the privy? Should I not be researching weightier matters?

There were threads in my childhood which set in motion the book you are now reading. Henry Woods, my great grandfather, died in 1886 of septicaemia, as a result of cutting himself emptying a bucket of night soil. This sad story was part of our family history and as a child I often wondered why night soil should be emptied, indeed what **was** night soil?

Henry was on my father's side but my mother's side was not without distinction. My mother's father lived with us and as an old man his great interest in life was the state of his bowels. Poppa's bowels were something that weighed heavily on me as a child. A great unspoken worry filled the house and I could sense adult unease if Poppa's bowels were not in full working order.

Over the years of work, marriage and children, my interest in lavatories, apart from keeping them clean, lapsed. Then about nine years ago I was asked to give a lecture on the History of Hygiene to students at my local College of Further Education, where I was a part-time lecturer. It changed my life.

Delving into the history of sanitation, I became fascinated

A delightful early 19th-century timber-framed, two-seater privy set in the heart of the Kent countryside near Benenden. Clad in weatherboarding with hipped tiled roof, a plank door and a small window, it was situated well away from the farmhouse, next to the pig sty, and known affectionately as 'the Office' or 'the Little house'.

with the social implications; the mundane act of defecation has wrought profound effects on every aspect of our social history. Dear Reader, I hope not to shock you but where to shit and what to do with it has occupied the minds of everyone down the ages, from the highest to the lowest in the land. It is our common bond, transcending class barriers, colour and creed. When the Prime Minister introduced the Public Health Act of 1875 with the historic words, 'Sanitas sanitatum, omnia sanitas', by gum we of the lower orders might not know what it meant, but we knew it would do us good.

Fired with a mission to explain, I have given talks all over Kent on the history of the bath and the lavatory, entitled 'Down the Pan'. Now I have been asked to put the fruits of my learning into this little book, it has not been easy.

The privies of Kent have all but disappeared. Why have the people of this county obliterated their recent sanitary past? The answer is that much of North Kent was heavily populated and we were in the forefront of the Sanitary Revolution. Main drainage and the destruction of the privy bucket was the gleam in every town councillor's eye.

Down on the south coast the lack of privy conservation was explained by Penny Ward, the Thanet Heritage Officer, 'Kent seaside areas relied on the holiday trade for their means before it was called the tourist industry. They were, therefore, very conscious of the risks involved in the collection of night soil and installed water closets very early. When children from Margate went to Staffordshire as evacuees in June 1940, they were taken aback at the privies which were quite unfamiliar to them.'

No use privy hunting there. So I turned inland, to the lovely countryside round Goudhurst, Benenden, Biddenden, Smarden, Cranbrook, the beautiful Elham Valley and there they were, the last precious few, waiting for me to discover them.

DULCIE LEWIS

The author looking into the subject of privies. A major 'find' in the churchyard at Selling inside was a beautifully preserved two-seater.

[1]

Privies Past

'Not to empty any privy or to remove Night Soil or empty Swine
Sties between 6 am and 11 am or deposit it in any street.'
(*Amendment to Rochester Bye-Laws 1842*)

It is my experience that at any social gathering where the topic
of Abroad comes up, it inevitably leads to stories of 'the horrors
of foreign lavatories'. Many an evening can be spent recounting
the beastliness of our European partners' 'arrangements'.
Indeed, we have come to view ourselves as world leaders when
it comes to the lavatory.

It was not always so. When the Romans landed in 55 BC in
Kent, on the beach between Deal and Walmer, they were
shocked at our sanitary provision — for we had none! It is not
actually recorded whether Julius Caesar asked for the bathroom, but if he had done, there would have been some blank
looks from the natives of Kent.

You could forgive the Romans for turning back and going
home. What on earth had been going on here? We had given no
thought to the disposal of our human waste and other rubbish.
Whilst the nearest stream was good enough for us, other civiliza-
tions had planned their hygiene affairs thoroughly.

We know that the ancient Egyptians as far back as 2900 BC
had strict rules about sanitation. The sanitary engineering of
the Minoans in the Crete of 2000 BC, with flowing water,
wooden seats and earthenware pan, surpassed anything we
were going to have until Victorian times. The people of Babylon,

11

the Greeks, certainly the Jews and the Romans, all gave a great deal of thought to their drains.

The Romans came to have another go at us in AD 43 and this time were not put off. Back home they were used to every sanitary amenity: aqueducts, hot and cold water, flowing water for waste disposal, filtered drinking water, public latrines, baths, drains and sewers. The public latrines had luxurious marble seats open to view and underneath there were troughs of flowing water for waste disposal — 'a place of easement', somewhere to linger and exchange the gossip of the day. The household gods of a Roman family included Stercutius, the god of manure and Cloacina, the goddess of sewers. These things mattered to the Romans.

Once settled here, the Romans built their villas, like Lullingstone near Eynsford, self contained little communities fending off the filthy savage. Your ordinary soldier was not left out of these provisions. Housesteads on Hadrian's Wall served to comfort the military with a bath-house and a latrine 31 ft long on which up to 20 men could sit at the end of a hard day guarding the frontier. The Romans were here for 400 years and tried to clean us up but we were having none of their funny foreign habits.

We remained in sanitary darkness for another 600 years, the Dark Ages, looking then to the Church for guidance. By 1150 the monks of the monastery of Christchurch in Canterbury were setting an example with a highly developed water system. Indeed, when the Black Death struck in 1349 the monks were spared, which could have been due either to the power of prayer or the efficacy of the drains.

A monastic life was ruled by the offices of the day and adequate arrangements had to be made when large numbers of men were likely to converge on the reredorter or privy at the back of the monastic dormitory. A good watercourse, supplemented by water from the roof, flushed the great drain under the reredorter out into the town ditch.

Would that sanitation had been so well ordered elsewhere. Privies were built into the thickness of the wall of the great house or castle. Known as garderobes, they consisted of a stone or wooden seat built over a shaft, which discharged into a cesspit, moat or ditch at the base of the tower. Other less private means of disposal would have a vent to the outside leaving the waste to trickle down the castle walls.

What of the rest of us? In towns there were a few public latrines, mostly built over rivers. London's watercourses suffered particularly badly and the Thames was already an open sewer. London Bridge had 138 houses built on it and 1 public privy — imagine the queues in the morning! It was easier and quicker to make other arrangements and the bridge was said to be 'for wise men to go over and for fools to go under'.

Something had to be done and the coming of the Black Death, carrying off a third of England's population, concentrated the mind. Street cleaning and tighter laws on privy building were introduced; overhanging latrines discharging into the street below were seen as a bad thing, at last! Cesspits were built where the waste from privies and latrines could be emptied.

Every age has its heroes and those of the 14th century were the rakers or gongfermors who had the unenviable job of cleaning out the privies and cesspits ('gong' from the Saxon 'gang', meaning 'to go off' and 'fermor' from 'fey', 'to cleanse'). They were rewarded handsomely, 'ye caryyng a way of a ton of dounge, 17 shillings.' Two local boys at Queenborough on the Isle of Sheppey who cleaned out the cesspit at the castle were aptly named William Mokkyng and Nicholas Richandgood.

Sadly, it all proved too little. The preferred method was still to empty the 'pysse potte' out of the bedroom window onto the street below. Here is the good Dr Boorde warning 'Beware of

A garderobe chute built in 1127 at Rochester Castle. The walls of this fine castle were not always so clean! In 1416 Sigismund, the Emperor of Germany, came to call bringing 1,000 knights, 1,000 squires, horses etc. How did the 7 garderobes cope with this influx?

Upnor Castle, built between 1559 and 1567 to protect the fleet anchored on the river Medway and the new dockyard in Chatham. Improved garderobes in the towers had drain shafts giving a clean drop into the river. Note the little 'keyhole' window in the tower to help with ventilation. Much nicer.

draughty privys and of pyssynne in draughts...Beware of emptyng pysse pottes, and pyssing in chymnes'.

For rich people, draughty garderobes were replaced by close stools. They were certainly more comfortable for the user but still unpleasant for those who emptied them. The close stool was a box with a lid, covered with velvet or other fine material and decorated with ribbons, gilt nails and fringes. It contained a pot and had a padded seat filled with horsehair or down. Henry VIII kept his in a private room off the State Bedchamber known as the Stool Room. His pewter pot was emptied by the influential Groom of the Stool, who was much concerned that His Majesty should have 'a very fair seige'.

Into this miasma of muck stepped Sir John Harington, godson of Queen Elizabeth I. He invented a flushing water closet and Her Majesty had one installed in Richmond Palace. It was not a great success and no one else seemed to see the exciting possibilities of the invention. Sadly, Sir John was 200 years too early.

There were odd 'sightings' of water closets over the next century. Queen Anne in the early 1700s had 'a closet that leads to a little place of easement of marble with sluices of water to wash all down'. Country people had no need of such things as the fields and woods provided for their needs but in the towns most only aspired to the chamber pot and the slop pail. Streets and alleys would echo to the sound of 'gardy-loo' (gardez-l'eau), 'watch out for the water', as out of the window went the contents of these receptacles. The social convention that a gentleman should walk on the outside of the pavement must surely come from these times; he could bear the brunt of whatever came from above.

Relief was in sight for amidst all this filth came one Alexander Cummings, a watchmaker, who patented a valve water closet in 1775. The water came from an overhead cistern and was kept in the pan by a sliding valve operated by a pull-up handle. Three

The lovely Restoration House in Rochester, built in 1587 and visited by Charles II in 1660. Wind holes ventilated the garderobes on the corner of the house and you can see a large opening for waste matter at the bottom.

An invention that did not need water was the earth closet patented by the Reverend Henry Moule in 1860. This unexpected 'find' in the grounds of Cooling Castle shows a wooden frame with a seat and hopper behind for the dry earth, charcoal or ashes. A pull of the handle in the seat released the earth onto the contents of the bucket. A family of six would use 2.5 tons of earth a year. Properly maintained, this method was quite hygienic and not smelly.

The 'Moule' at Cooling Castle.

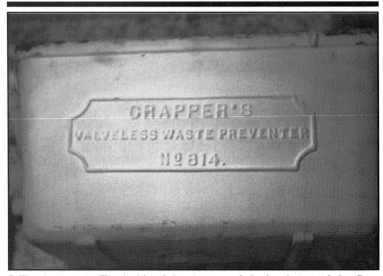

Still going strong! The inside of the cistern and the bowl, named the 'Largarea', have had to be replaced but Patrick and Anne Hills of Chiddingstone Causeway are very happy with their 'Crapper'.

years later Joseph Bramah, a cabinet maker, greatly improved Cummings' model, notably with a hinged valve. By 1797 Bramah had made 6,000 closets and the workmanship was so high that his name passed into the English language, 'bramah' meaning something really good.

There were other water closets, like the pan closet around 1780, flushed by pouring a jug of water. The long hopper of the 1850s flushed from the top with a thin spiral of water that 'by the time it has twirled itself down to the trap it has no energy left to carry anything with it'. Competitions were held to find the most efficient water closet; most failed on the strength of the flush.

The Public Health Act of 1848 made it law that a fixed sanitary arrangement, whether it was an earth closet, a privy, a water closet or a bucket must be fitted to every household. The race was on. Many of those Victorian sanitary engineers are

A typical brick-built privy under a peg-tile roof behind a cottage near Cran-brook. Once a common sight, now so often a tool shed. This one, however, still contains a two-holer (not in use).

remembered even now, their names enshrined in our lavatory bowls: Sir Henry Doulton, Mr Thomas Twyford, Mr Shanks and of course Mr Thomas Crapper.

It was Thomas Crapper at his Marlborough Works in Chelsea who refined and perfected the water cistern. His Crapper's Valveless Waste Preventer was pioneered as a result of government legislation in 1872 to cut down on the shocking waste of water due to dodgy valves. We have the Americans to thank for taking Mr Crapper's name back to America after World War I and using it so effectively when visiting the lavatory. Mr Crapper died in 1910 and is buried in Beckenham, Kent.

These pioneering gentlemen helped the 'big push' for flush water closets in towns that went on apace from the turn of this century. But what of the country dwellers? How did those not blessed with main drainage fare? Let us examine some particular privies here in Kent and savour the stories and mishaps that occurred on taking a walk to the bottom of the garden.

[2]

PARTICULAR PRIVIES

I must down to the privy again,
To the lonely loo and the sky,
And all I ask is a warm seat
And some paper to wipe me dry,
And the cobwebs cling and the draughts sing -
And the old door creaking,
And a wet patch on my bald head
As the roof above is leaking.

(*Apologies to John Masefield*)

Sitting on our modern, easy flush lavatory, it is hard to imagine the difficulties surrounding defecation endured by generations still living to tell the tale. Today we can pop to our downstairs cloakroom, bathroom or 'ensuite facilities' without ever leaving the comfort of the central heating.

All the lovely letters I received when I first started this book show it was quite different not so long ago. In certain weather conditions a trip to the privy could require heavy duty clothes, an umbrella, wellingtons, a light and more often than not a companion to ward off the silent shadows of the night.

The first thing to remember about a good privy was that it should be built some distance from the house. Far better to have a brisk walk to the bottom of the garden than have the privy within sniffing distance of the house.

Eileen Chittenden of Great Chart recalls the journey to the privy. 'I was born in the small village of Bonnington on the edge of Romney Marsh in 1932. We had a very long garden

A single-seater privy tucked in the wall at the bottom of the garden and a good distance from the house, which is in Charing High Street and dates back to the 15th century. The white stuff is snow, reminding us just how uncomfortably cold it must have been!

24

with a winding path leading to a little wooden hut, the dunnikin, in amongst trees at the end. It had a wooden seat with a hole and a bucket underneath. There was a small door in the front of the seat for removal of the bucket and my father used to dig a hole in his garden and empty the contents. He grew wonderful vegetables! In the winter when it was dark and wet, I remember dressing up in rainwear, wellies and a torch to pay a visit.'

Sandra remembers her Kent childhood between 1946 and 1964 on the Isle of Oxney. 'We had a two-seater loo, a real earth closet made of brick and tile. It was not just at the end of the garden but at right angles so that when in there you lost sight of the house, very nerve racking at night. A lovely white rose grew by it. I remember having to walk past bushes and coming in with a caterpillar on my nightdress.'

Sometimes you combined a short walk and a climb into your trip to the privy. Mrs Pam Simmonds lived 'with my husband's family in London Road, Sevenoaks, just after the war. The houses were built into a hill and the loo was reached by going through the kitchen, out of the house, across a yard, up a flight of cement steps (by which time you were level with the bedrooms) and into a small garden. A kind of workmen's hut of horizontal wooden slats housed a high level, flush water lavatory. A torch, hat and umbrella were essential for this journey. There was no electricity in there but you did have the most magnificent view over Polhill towards Bromley. I called it the Eagle's Nest.'

Privies could be brick built, wooden, corrugated tin or hidden in outbuildings or 'lodges' as they were sometimes called. Inside, the brickwork was plastered and then whitewashed, limewashed or painted a mid blue. The colour blue repelled the flies!

People did their best to disguise the nature of the building with climbing roses and sweet smelling honeysuckle up and over the

A former two-holer privy behind an 18th-century cottage in Biddenden.
Delightfully camouflaged with a riot of foliage.

A brick-built privy at the bottom of the garden behind the 17th-century Black Lion in Lynsted. Once used as a 'ladies', it shelters under a huge yew tree.

A privy at Park Hill, Appledore. Common bond brickwork, a Kent peg-tile roof and lathe and plaster inside with traces of blue paint. The owner, Mrs Smith, has planted houseleeks on the roof; believed by the Greeks and Romans to protect a building from thunderbolts. Mrs Smith is taking no chances!

privy roof. Mr Welland of Minster remembers a two-holer with 'an elder bush on one side and a mass of summer jasmine all over the top, sparkling with white stars and heavy with perfume.' Certainly the dense foliage of privet hid the sight and muffled the sounds of what was going on within. Many privies I photographed had a yew tree growing nearby. It was thought years ago that the guardian spirit of the house lived in the yew. Dire things were said to happen to those who felled the yew, so often the privy was pulled down but the tree remained.

You were never far from nature in a privy. Mrs Susie Filmer of Shadoxhurst had a 'dunnakin' with a date carved inside of 1700. 'It was 50 feet down the garden path near our garden gate. There it was a bit on the skew and the door went the same way

— no bolt or handle to fix it. It was built of heavy oak pieces with large cracks and holes to give plenty of sunlight or moonshine. Inside was a heavy pole to hold fast for comfort, a long string holding the "not so soft" newspaper squares and an out of date calendar. The spiders would be there, waiting to scare, father would tell us the cobwebs kept it warm! My two sisters always seemed to hold on until dark and the moon would light our way on the brick path, me holding the lighted candle in a jam jar as we made our way through the cold, wet or fog. Outside grew hollyhocks and brambles and an old bullace (wild damson) tree holding the privy up, with plenty of tasty ripe fruit.'

Margaret Fenn of Littlebourne WI recalls a cousin who many years ago lived in a cottage at Pett Bottom, near Canterbury. Their privy was built under a plum tree and at the right time of the year they could sit in there quite happily and listen to the ripe plums hitting the corrugated tin roof.

Ellen Excell of Sevenoaks remembers living in a farm cottage in Benover, near Yalding, where the earth closet was at the bottom of the garden under an old quince tree. 'I've never managed to make such delicious quince jam as Mum made.'

Dorothy James of East Stourmouth paints a vivid picture of the trip down the garden path and the dangers awaiting. 'Over 40 years ago when I was a 10 year old girl I used to visit my Grandfather White. His old thatched cottage had no plumbing at all so while I was there I would use the ivy-clad privy at the bottom of the garden. It was reached by a long, cinder path that edged a well tended vegetable garden. Little did I know at the time what made the greens so lush and the peas so sweet. His home-made compost was a mystery to me.

'Behind "The Closet" lurked "The Poke Hole". This was a shallow pit about 6 feet wide, in which Granddad rotted down all his garden rubbish and household waste for mulching his garden. Into this pit he also emptied the contents of "The

Better than a candle in a jam jar - a paraffin lamp you could keep in the privy to lighten the darkness (Brattle Farm Museum at Staplehurst).

Closet" pail. During the hot weather the mixture fermented well, forming a thick crust on top. One day I was tempted to walk across it but the crust gave way in the centre. I had to squelch back down the cinder path calling for a bucket of water to clean my face and legs. Happy days!'

Nowadays we are obsessed with privacy. There was no place for social niceties in an outdoor privy. If it was cold, dark and wet you needed to go quickly, preferably with someone to keep you company. You might have a candle or even a paraffin lamp but the shadows in the corners played on the imagination and one needed the comfort of another presence. An older member of the family was forced to go down the garden path to supervise a younger sibling. This caused untold resentment and much time wasting by younger children as sweet revenge for some unfairness they felt had been done to them. If one could time the visit to the privy at just the moment an older sister was all dressed up to go out, all well and good.

One old lady now in her mid 80s wrote to me about her outdoor privy during the First World War. 'We would have a candle in a jam jar for lighting in the dark evenings. My younger brother would accompany me and swing on the wooden door while I was "occupied" and vice versa.'

Not every family could afford the luxury of a candle and Margaret Hourigan of Chatham can remember visits as a little girl to an aunt living in Luton and her mother standing at the back door shouting encouragement as she plunged on down the garden path into the enveloping darkness.

The story is told of a young girl, brought up in the town, on her honeymoon with her new husband. To save money they stayed with his relations in the country. On the first night faced with the outside privy, and unused to such things, the young bride insisted that her new husband sit by her side.

It was not unusual to accompany a loved one to the privy. I was told of Mabel and Fred of Five Oak Green who, newly married, would walk down the garden path, hand in hand, to the privy. It was always a matter of considerable conjecture to the children next door whether they sat side by side still holding hands.

Sometimes you could be faced with unwanted, even unexpected, company. Margaret Hourigan recalls her mother as a young woman going out to the privy and finding a tramp asleep, propped up on the seat. The door was kept locked thereafter.

Seating numbers in a privy depended very much on family size. A two-holer privy seat was common, often with the second hole smaller and set lower for children. Mrs Pretious of Northfleet recalls just such a two-holer in a farm cottage at Clements Reach, near Meopham, in the 1920s. 'It had buckets underneath which were emptied 3 or 4 times a week from a door at

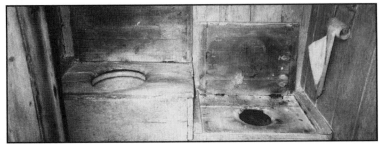

A two-holer complete with lids, with one seat lower for a child, behind a house in Charing. The privy backs onto the wall surrounding the remains of the Archbishop's Palace. Earthenware bowls, flushed to the other side of the wall with a jug of water. The toilet roll holder is modestly named 'La Première'.

the back. It backed onto a cattle yard — all very nice on a hot summer's day.'

Ellen Excell tells of another farm cottage, this time at Brenchley, near Yalding, that had a two-holer, one large and one small for children. 'I remember a small shelf on the wall holding a candle and a box of matches. I only had use for them when it was my turn to escort my scared London cousins to the privy in the dark.'

If our present day need for privacy is repelled by the thought of a two-holer, imagine a three-holer! A large family might well find the need for this facility, certainly I have heard tell of such things in old pubs and inns. Ruth Gray remembers her childhood fascination in the 1920s with a three-holer. 'I was just 6 when we had to move from our nice little house with a flush toilet to a converted chapel house in Stelling Minnis. On being introduced to the three-holer (all different sizes) I remarked, "It must be for the three bears! Look, large for Father Bear, medium for Mother Bear and small for Baby Bear."'

This magnificent three-holer had the added advantage of being easily moved — a kind of forerunner of today's portaloo. 'The little hut had a handle either end and was moved and placed over a new trench when the old one was full. A bucket of earth was to hand to sprinkle over waste matter, as required. We always grew elder bushes nearby to deter the flies!' One can imagine this little privy being moved round the garden, taking advantage of the early morning sun, the scent of roses at dusk or even placed where the soil needed enriching.

In a row of terraced houses or cottages the privies at the bottom of the garden could be joined as well. If you were friends with your neighbours all well and good, you could leave the door open, enjoy a chat and a bit of gossip, whilst attending to the call of nature. Young people liked this sociable aspect; often laughter and singing could be heard at the bottom of the garden. Others

Privies behind a row of pretty terraced cottages in St Peter's, Broadstairs. The cottages and the privies were originally for the servants of 'the Big House'.

not so fortunate had to actually share a privy with next door. A kind of social etiquette was observed, especially if it were a two-holer. Each family would stick to their own hole with both families owning a key and the privy always kept locked.

It was difficult if you fell out with the neighbours — after all it was not easy sharing these arrangements when you had just had a blazing row. A story told at the Pandora Club in Gillingham after one of my talks illustrates this.

Two families living in Gillingham shared a two-holer at the bottom of the garden. This privy had a deep pit that only needed clearing out once a year. They fell out, and one family took themselves off in a huff to make their own privy arrangements. This involved using sacking to screen off a bucket in their garden shed. Later they rigged up a seat but still they had nowhere to empty the bucket. Father was to be seen constantly digging his small garden in an effort to rid himself of the family waste. Imagine the fury and indignation at every bucketful. Cutting off one's privy to spite one's bottom!

Again at the Pandora Club I was told of a childhood in a little cottage close to the Sittingbourne Paper Mills. 'After the First World War my father had to leave London to seek work. We had been used to indoor flush lavatories and this was a bit of a come-down. You went down the garden, across a path at the back of the gardens, to the privies. You had to carry a pail of water with you, to flush the privy and as the fences were low between the gardens everyone could see where you were going and the purpose of your visit.'

There was not much chance of privacy for Mary Wallace of East Malling and her devoted dog, who 'every time I went down the garden came with me and sat outside the privy. If anyone called while I was down there, he would bark and everyone knew what I was doing.'

It was not uncommon for town relations to look askance at

their country cousins' arrangements and it cannot have been easy making a visit. Molly Young writes movingly of the horrors that awaited her back in the 1920s when she left the sophistication and comforts of Canterbury for a holiday.

'As a small child living in Canterbury we had a water closet. My relations lived mostly in the country and I loved going to stay with them in the summer holidays, except for having to use the awful pail lavatories. Most were housed in a wooden hut, a big wooden seat with a hole in the centre and some with two holes, the second one smaller for a child — all of them occupied by hundreds of spiders, which I feared more than anything. They were very clean, with religious texts on the walls and squares of newspaper hung by a string from a nail in the wall. These privies were right at the bottom of the garden, on a pouring wet night it was a nightmare getting to it.

'When we visited my father's sister I had to be especially careful as her earth closet had no bucket and you were sitting over a very large pit. I was taught to hold on tightly to the edge of the seat or you would disappear.'

Things did not get any better for Molly as she grew up. 'When I was first married we had a walk to the end of the garden, turn right into a field and quite a little way along. It felt quite lonely sitting out there. This was the only privy I have ever seen with a diamond-shaped hole — I think a man must have designed it for his own comfort. I hated them one and all.'

Frances Carr remembers her brother, who married a Chatham girl, bringing his new wife to the family farmhouse. 'She was petrified on realising that the lavatory was a two-holer across the farmyard.'

The owner can remember when her girl cousins from the town came to stay. Her brother, a great tease, would bang on the door and sides to frighten them, especially when it was dark. 'The town cousins thought we were a bit basic but I always felt we were a lot better off as they used to carry their waste bucket through the house.'

My teenage years in the 1950s were spent in the country at Borden, near Sittingbourne. In spite of my interest in the subject, I have to admit we never had a privy. However, my friend in Sittingbourne did have one. She and her mother ignored this brick-built building halfway down the garden and visitors would be offered a commode in the bedroom. All around neighbours were applying for grants towards indoor bathrooms but her father saw no reason to change. I saw it as an act of friendship never to ask for the lavatory when at her house and would hang on until I was bursting, when I would peddle as fast as I could the two miles home. Often I did not make it and went behind a hedge. Still our friendship remained intact.

What my family used was an old, high level, cast iron, flush lavatory, just along from the back door. I quite liked going outside to the lavatory for it was the perfect place to day dream; peace and oneness with nature rarely captured since. Warm spring evenings meant sitting on the lavatory at dusk, looking beyond the yard to our orchard, seeing the cherry blossom luminous against the evening sky. The faint smell of mother's Consulate Menthol cigarettes that she smoked out there, combined with father's St Bruno pipe tobacco, giving a feeling of stability and rightness with the world — seminal, near perfect moments.

[3]

DOWN THE 'OLE

The privy hole is deep and vast,
Its unknown depths beware.
Both hands must clasp the board quite fast
Or greet its murky lair.

The privy seat was fraught with danger. A hole too large could
have far reaching consequences. A careless moment, an ill-
judged shift to the side, could see a precious item plunged on a
journey of no return. Decisions would have to be made: just
how badly did you want it back? On the whole, gloves were

A two-holer near Benenden dropping directly to the outside and ending up at
the back of the privy in a brick-lined pit.

Round the back.

best left where they lay. Livestock, on the other hand, was a different matter.

Mrs Bryan of Chatham remembers her early married life in the 1920s at Henry Street. 'We had a brick-built privy, two holes, one high, one low, built into a box over a deep pit. Aunt Trapp lived next door and had the same arrangement. She kept hens and a grumpy old cockerel in the backyard and every morning would let them out, "shooing" them down the garden to have a scratch about.

'Aunt Trapp's mother from Essex was staying and she went to use the privy in the yard. She came back indoors looking very worried, "I can't go in there, there's a funny noise down your hole." Aunt Trapp called me over the fence to come and have a look with her. We peered down that privy hole and there below, was the cockerel, perched as proud as you please on the pole that ran across the cesspit. When he was being "shooed" he must have gone off and flown down the hole. Anyway he had to stay there until night time when Mr Trapp got home.

'It wasn't easy rescuing that cockerel. First Mr Trapp had to move the big box from over the cesspit, then he lay down on the floor and waved his hands about below in the pit. All that did was set the cockerel a-dancing on the pole, still out of reach of Mr Trapp. There was nothing for it; calling to my husband to come and hold onto his ankles, Mr Trapp slowly lowered his body into the pit. You should have heard the noise, cockerel flapping his wings, Mr Trapp shouting not to let go and all the time that bird stirring up everything that was down there. He grabbed the cockerel eventually and hauled him up. I don't know who looked worse, the cockerel or Mr Trapp. Anyway the cockerel didn't seem to come to much harm — I'm not so sure about Mr Trapp.'

Another story of emerging unscathed from the privy is told by Mr Fred Holyer of Kingsnorth, Ashford. 'My grandfather had a

A privy near Frittenden, possibly just for the men of the farm. It would have been a foolish small child who sat on this seat for the hole is extremely large.

two-seater at his farm in Old Romney in Romney Marsh. It was a tarred building about 25 yards from the back door and called the "back-house". It had a large hole and a smaller one on a lower level for children. One of my uncles used to dance on the seat and one day fell through the large hole. He would have been about three at the time. His mother heard his screams and managed to pull him out from the back, where there was a flap for emptying. Of the four boys in the family, he grew the tallest and lived the longest, into his 90s. So it did him no harm!'

Boys will be boys, as a story heard at Upchurch Wives Group goes to show. 'My younger brother was a right pain. He would never go down the garden on his own — I always had to go with him and usually I had better things to do. We had a big hole and a little hole lower down. He always wanted to go on the big hole but wasn't supposed to. One day I had had enough. He started whining to sit on the big hole, so I said, "Fair enough" and lifted

42

Altogether safer, a two-holer with buckets in a privy near Hever has an adult hole and a smaller one for a child.

him up and pushed him down firmly through the big hole. There he was doubled up with his little legs sticking straight up in front of him. Well I left him there, shouting his head off. Of course, Mum came and pulled him out and I got a thick ear. Mind you, he didn't seem to want me to go with him quite so often after that.'

Not so very dreadful, but consider the following told to me by Patrick and Anne Hills of Chiddingstone Causeway:

There was a young fellow called Hyde
Who fell down a privy and died.
His unfortunate brother
Then fell down another
And now they're interred side by side.

43

I heard the next story while walking in the Elham Valley. Tom, Harry and their friend 'Orsemuck had been out drinking one Saturday night. A few beers too many saw the lads bouncing off the hedges as they made their way home. As they arrived at Tom's little cottage first he invited them to go no further but to sleep it off in his front room.

During the night Harry felt a bit queer and needed to 'go'. grabbing a torch from the kitchen table, he made his way unsteadily out of the back door, up the garden path and into Tom's privy. 'This torch is handy,' thought Harry, placing it down beside him. He was soon back indoors in the warm. Soon afterwards 'Orsemuck had a pressing need to 'go' as well. Staggering up the garden path, he could see a faint glow from under the privy door.

'That's kind of old Tom to leave a light on in there,' thought 'Orsemuck. It's even better inside, for a beautiful white light shines upwards from the privy hole.

'Well,' said 'Orsemuck, settling down on the seat, 'Old Tom must be doing well for 'isself — I ain't got 'lectric in my lav.'

The next morning the three pals were nursing their hangovers when 'Orsemuck said, 'Ere, I ain't seen one of those fancy privy lights afore — must have set you back a bit.'

'What light?' said Tom. 'There ain't no light in my privy 'cept a bit of moonlight.'

The horrible truth dawned on Harry and, looking at his friend, he said sheepishly, 'You know that new torch of yourn...' and 'You could have told me you'd got two holes.'

You do not have to be drunk to be careless. Here is Mrs Marlene Neep remembering a story her mother told her of when she was a child in the early 1920s. 'Grandma had a two-holer privy — one for the adults and next to it a smaller one for the children. One day a lady visitor trotted off down the garden to the "lav", still wearing white gloves. She removed them as she sat down,

44

and placed them next to her, only to discover that they had disappeared down the children's hole. She returned to the house ungloved — thank goodness.'

Mrs Leonard of Pluckley reflects on a privy that has seen more that its fair share of action. 'I moved from Hastingleigh to Bethersden in 1914. We had a three-seater outside privy at Dyne's Farm. It was for a grown up and two smaller holes for children. Over the years the seat had become very warped.

'One snowy winter's day one of the cats came indoors and we could smell something terrible. The cat had sat on the privy seat and fallen in! Mum had to bath her. This happened during the First World War. Over 20 years later my sister and her husband moved in and that seat was still warped.

'One day during the Second World War they were down the fields working. It was the day the butcher's boy delivered the meat ration. So on the path by the front door my sister put out a huge earthenware crock and on the lid she wrote "Butcher, please leave meat in the crock." When they got back from the fields they could not find the meat anywhere. So they asked a neighbour if they had had their meat delivered. "Yes," says the neighbour, "and I saw the lad going up your path." They searched everywhere but could not find the meat, until, that is, someone needed to go to the privy. The butcher's boy had left the meat on the privy seat and, it being so twisted, the meat had fallen into the bucket! So they told the butcher the meat was lost. He said, "I've sacked that lad, he's just tied a string of sausages to another customer's door handle and the cat has had them." Luckily the butcher could see the funny side of it and replaced the meat.

'Incidentally, the fish in the pond enjoyed the meat from the privy.'

Mrs Leonard also recalls that whilst things do tend to go down the hole, sometimes things come up it too. 'My late husband lived in Pluckley close to the Blacksmith's Arms. When he was about 10 years old, he was very friendly with the landlord's son who was "sweet" on a girl living next door to my husband. They all had privies out the back with cesspits, with a door at the back for emptying. Thinking it was the girl sitting on the privy, my hubby and his friend put a stinging nettle through the door and up the hole. Unfortunately it was her dad sitting there. He chased them across the fields but he couldn't catch them. However my hubby got the good hiding when he returned home, he never forgot it!'

[4]

SOME QUESTIONS ANSWERED — ON PAPER

There once was an expert on loos,
Who on paper had very strong views.
From the privy he'd come
With print on his bum,
Once again, all behind with the news.

The simple act of bottom wiping — a humble action and not often remarked on, but how used we to manage? Nowadays we have our pastel, soft, even patterned, lavatory paper conveniently to hand, but it was not always so.

Paper has been around for centuries, but was not used for such purposes. The Romans, as usual, led the way, favouring a stick with a sponge on the end, like a small spear — but without the pointy bit! There would be several in their public lavatories and, after using one, the thoughtful Roman would wash the stick with the sponge in a trough of salt water and leave it, ready for the next person to use. Hence the expression 'To get hold of the wrong end of the stick!'

In Britain the early monks used old habits, torn up. The rest of us favoured bunches of hay on the end of a curved stick, stones that were flat and smooth, grass, handfuls of herbs and leaves. A bundle of dock leaves by the privy door was always prudent.

I am grateful to Mr T. O'Leary of Rainham for reminding me of this historical snippet:

In days of old
When knights were bold
And paper weren't invented
They wiped their arse
With blades of grass,
And walked away contented.

There were some grand folk like the Earl of Chesterfield who recommended to his son that he tear out a couple of pages from a poetry book, take them with him to the 'necessary-house', read them there and then use them. 'It is better than only doing what you cannot help doing at those moments and it will make any book which you shall read in that manner, very present to your mind.'

Squares of lavatory paper were used as a preventative against

A very superior lavatory paper holder, 'The Crown Toilet Fixture', found at Gads Hill, Higham. The house was owned by Charles Dickens until his death in 1870 and is now a private school.

piles in 1857 but the roll came later when the British Patent Perforated Paper Company started manufacturing in 1880. However, it is obvious from the many letters I received on the subject, that lavatory paper, as we know it, was not part of the furnishings of most Kent privies. In the Medway Towns people often made use of 'tow', fibres of hemp, which filled the joints on the decks of ships. But the most favoured lavatory paper of all was — newspaper squares.

Mr R. Waters of Aldington, near Ashford, remembers his two-holer 'dunnakin'. 'I lived in a farm cottage at Lympne from the time I was born until I was 26 years old. I am now 82 and your letter brought back many memories. Toilet paper was newspaper cut into squares. A hole made in one corner and string put through to hang it up on a nail. The only thing was, you got a black bum as the ink came off the newspaper and you had to sit and rub it in your hands to make it soft.'

Country privies reflected country matters. Peggy Fryer of Cranbrook remembers 'visiting some farming friends when I was a little girl in the early 1930s. They had a privy up the garden and the "paper" was torn sheets of the *Farmer and Stockbreeder* and, being a farmer's daughter, I had to read each bit before using it.'

Mrs Marjorie Short in her days in the Women's Land Army used the torn up pages of the *Farmers Weekly*.

The *Daily Mail* seems to have been a favourite; many have testified to me that its ink did not come off. Ray Christopher of the *Medway News* vouchsafed that abroad in the Army the airmail edition of *The Times* was much sought after; delivering a very soft, thorough wipe. The *News of the World* was often on hand but was heavily censored by mother, as the racier articles were always missing.

A different kind of censorship is recalled by Mrs Bryan of Chatham. 'Back in 1906 when I was a little girl I was not allowed to

You could always improve your mind while you were waiting for nature to take its course! (*See also* 'Lucy's loo' in chapter 5.)

A selection of china chamber pots from the Brattle Farm Museum at Staplehurst.

read the newspaper as my father wanted to keep things from me. My teacher said to me that I should improve my reading by reading the newspaper; father was horrified. So I used to go into the dunnikin and read the squares and he wouldn't know.'

If you were unlucky enough to run out of newspaper, as often happened in a large family, brown wrapping paper could be substituted. It was not as good, but needs must ... Reserved as a special treat for visitors would be the squares of paper in which oranges used to be wrapped, soft and not unlike tissue.

The job of keeping the privy fully supplied with newspaper squares was often delegated to a child. Mr Crook of Walderslade recalls Saturday morning duties. 'Back in the 1920s when I was about 6 years old, my job was to cut up the newspaper squares to Mother's exact specification. You had to make a hole with a meat skewer and pull the string through. There were a couple

51

of hooks in the privy and I had to fill these hooks. Then one day Mother said that I didn't have to do it any more; we were not having squares. She didn't seem very pleased as there was going to be extra expense.

'According to Mother there was a countrywide epidemic of bottom rashes. It was so bad there had even been Questions in the House of Commons! As a result the Government enforced all paper making factories to produce a percentage of their output in the form of toilet rolls.

'My mother was very proud to have lived during a time of great changes, the most exciting of which was the development of the internal combustion engine. I tell my grandson that I too have lived through exciting times — lavatory paper for all!'

Finally, for those seeking a crushing reply to the tiresome letters sent to us by officialdom:

'I have your letter before me and it will soon be behind me.'

[5]

How To Avoid Being 'Indelicate'

If you want a pee	You can go for a wash,
There's the WC	If you want to be posh.
You can pluck a rose	Retire, take your ease,
Or powder your nose,	Do as you please.
And sit on the throne,	What's in a name —
Whilst being alone.	The meaning's the same.

What to call it? On those occasions when we need to ask for 'the facilities', we tend to employ a euphemism or circumlocutory language. In polite society we are anxious not to offend with what we have come to think of as crude speech or coarse words. The act of defecation, the repository for our efforts and their disposal, cause us to bend and twist the English language. Even I am falling into the trap of obfuscation in my efforts not to offend the Reader's sensibilities — but enough of this. What I am trying to say is that we do not like calling a spade a spade.

Here is the kind of mess you find yourself in when trying not to be 'indelicate'. A foreigner visiting this country for the first time and straight off the boat at Dover, decided to stop in Canterbury. In need of refreshment as well as the lavatory he entered a pretty little cafe and seated himself at a table. There was a particularly dozy waitress serving that day. The foreigner placed his order with the waitress, but having other pressing needs and knowing that not all our words for the lavatory were socially acceptable, he decided to play safe. 'Excuse me, Miss,' he said to the waitress, 'Do you have a cloakroom?' 'No,' she replied, 'but you can use the hat stand.'

Is it embarrassment that causes us to cloak the simple request, 'I need to use the lavatory' in such ambiguous language? Instead of coming straight out with it we ask to:

Spend a penny	Wash our hands
Check the moorings	Stretch our legs
Be excused	See a man about a dog
Check the plumbing	Turn our bicycle around

Indeed one writer told me of an aunt back in the 1930s who had opted for town life — much to the disgust of her family in the country. She was thought to regard herself as a trifle superior, for she had lost her taste for collective stool-passing on the family two-holer when she came visiting. On one occasion, much as she tried to control her bladder, the quantity of cider consumed proved overwhelming. She disdained to use the privy, saying she preferred 'a gypsy's kiss', and relieved herself behind the red currant bushes.

A friend, Barbara Amos, supplied me with the Cockney rhyming slang for lavatory, 'family tree'. Hence the expression 'I'm just going to water the family tree'.

We have all been in houses where the lavatory door sports one of those delicate little china plaques bearing the words: 'Here it is' or 'The wee hoosie' or, even more twee, 'The Powder Room'. Even if we are so bold as to put up the word 'lavatory' on the door, that in itself is a euphemism. In medieval times 'the laver' or lavatory in the monastery or castle was the stone trough in which hands were washed, the word 'laver' in French meaning 'to wash'. The privy of those times was called 'the necessarium' or 'necessary house' and even the word 'garderobe' really meant 'wardrobe', just as we would use 'cloakroom', when the last thing on our mind was storing our cloaks.

Coy evasions are not a recent thing. The monks of Christchurch in Canterbury called their communal privy or reredorter, 'the third dormitory' — thought by some to be linked to the monks' habit of dozing off within its recesses! Echoes of the word 'reredorter' reach us from the past, as I was reliably informed that in the 1930s schoolboys at King's School in Canterbury referred to the lavatory as 'going to the reres'.

In the 1700s the privy could be the 'house of office', a 'convenience' or, to our minds a bit cruder but perfectly acceptable then, a 'bog house'. To use any of these outside privies a lady would always 'be at pains of stepping into the garden to pluck a rose'.

The Victorians favoured the euphemistic 'water closet', shortened to WC. This abbreviation has often caused problems. I heard the story of a Welsh farmer replying to a Gillingham lady enquiring about the WC attached to a holiday cottage on his farm. Thinking she must be a devout churchgoer, he mistook WC to mean Wesleyan Chapel and replied as follows:

The WC is situated about ten miles from your cottage, in beautiful scenery and is open the second and fourth Sunday in the month only. I am sorry it is not open more often, especially if you are used to going regularly. However people come from miles around and have a picnic afterwards. It is always busy in the summer and I do advise you to get there early as seating is limited to 60 but you can always stand at the back. On some Sundays you can go in early and there is an organ recital which is very popular.

When you arrive my wife will draw you a map showing you how to get there. We have been so busy recently we have not been able to go ourselves and this distresses us very much. It is our intention to go again one day.

With best wishes...

Lucy's loo at Staplehurst with the 1957 *Daily Mail*. This newspaper was a great favourite as it did not leave newsprint on the bottom!

A high level, cast iron WC in the garden of a house at Newington. 'The Storm King' promised a powerful flush.

It would be an unwise parent who gave a child names with the initials W and C. Many people have told me that Winston Churchill refused to have his initials on any of his offices, but how true that is I cannot say.

Many of us use the word 'loo' and this is thought to come from the French 'lieux d'aisance', meaning water closet. However, as Fred Nixon, the Editor of *Kent — Magazine of the County Society*, pointed out to me, 'lew' and 'loo' were old Kent words for 'sheltered place'.

Some people prefer the word 'toilet'. A trip to photograph Lucy's loo at Staplehurst reminded me of how once even 'toilet' was regarded as not quite correct. Lucy's loo, behind a 17th-century cottage, was an old cast iron, high flush, outside privy, not used for years. Lucy. newly moved in, had not had time to do anything about it. To our delight we found an old *Daily Mail* dated 24 October 1957 stuffed behind the pan, obviously put there as reserve lavatory paper.

All the famous people of the day were there: Macmillan and Eisenhower, Prince Rainier taking Grace out to dinner, and Nancy Mitford. I chuckled to think they had been behind that lavatory pan for over 40 years, especially Nancy Mitford. It was she who in the 1950s edited a book, *Noblesse Oblige*, about U and non-U language. U stood for upper class and it was the opinion put forward in this book that the word 'toilet paper' was terribly non-U but 'lavatory paper' was U; to refer to the WC was non-U and the U way to mention the lavatory was 'Let me show you the geography of the house'.

The Victorians liked the new water closets to have names that were majestic and grand. Thomas Crapper favoured Chelsea street names like Cadogan and Sloane, although I would have had doubts about sitting on his model named Shark! Other names reinforced the idea of a strong powerful flush — such as the Deluge, Torrent, Niagara — whereas the Rocket and the Thunderbox may be alluding to something altogether different!

So the purpose of the privy had to be wrapped up in the glories of the English language and the building camouflaged with sweet-smelling flowers, trees and bushes. 'Delicacy' did not stop there, however, for one elderly lady told me that as a young girl she was on the way to the privy and happened to be eating a piece of bread and jam at the time. Her mother called out crossly to her, 'What are you doing? Going in there and eating that, you are feeding the Devil and starving God!'

However lowly our purpose, once inside, beauty and pure thoughts must be the order of the day. Audrey Hooker from Egerton remembers: 'In the 1920s my grandparents lived in a small flint cottage, at Tunstall, near Sittingbourne. The two-holer earth closet was some distance away from the cottage. As a child I loved to visit Granny but I dreaded the long trek to the privy, especially in the dark carrying a candle in a jam jar.

'However, reassurance awaited because on opening the door of the privy, on the wall above the two privy seats hung a text, "HOME SWEET HOME". On the other wall hung a beautifully framed Victorian religious text:

> As pants the hart for cooling streams, when heated in the chase,
> So longs my soul, O God, for Thee, and thy refreshing Grace.

Obviously a bargain that Grandfather must have picked up at a sale — but so very appropriate.'

Not quite so high minded was Phyllis Edwards, who during the Second World War was living in Dover. 'When the shelling of Dover started my parents sent my sister and me to live with an auntie in the Alkham Valley. The toilet was an old earth closet with a wooden seat in a shed at the side of the garden, away from the house. It was one of my duties each week to scrub the toilet, my aunt always said how well I did it. To keep it looking nice we used to stick all the funny newspaper cuttings and birthday cards on the walls to read while waiting for relief.'

You could have lofty thoughts or quiet chuckles on your privy but some aspired to greater things. I am grateful to the Kent author Alan Major, whose memory of visits to his aunt at Chartham shows that 'delicacy' could be had within the walls of even an earth privy. 'Auntie's loo seemed to be the repository of all the pictures she had collected through married life, tired of and, having no attic or garden shed, had delegated to spend the rest of their existence on the walls of the building. A visitor could never be bored when having to use the loo. To a non-expert the closet was as good as the Tate Gallery! One could sit there for hours and enjoy again masterpieces of the past and see features that had not been noticed before.

'The majority were by hack artists of rocky shores, as little known as the artist who painted them by the dozen for a few shillings each. But there were copies of classics. *The Monarch of the Glen* proudly stood as firmly on the Highland soil in my Auntie's

59

loo as it had done in a million other Victorian homes. There were virtuous Victorian maidens piously rejecting the advances of male temptation, and a well-known scene of Thames barges in the red sunset. There were also long-dead faces of relatives, none of whom looked happy.'

What better place to reflect on the nature of sin, the weakness of the flesh and intimations of mortality? How many of us can say that the lavatory of today can measure up to the true 'delicacy' of Auntie's earth closet?

Looking down onto the remains of Cooling Castle - the 'loo with the view'. This substantial building housed an earth closet and the window ensured both light and fresh air.

[6]

NATURE IN ALL ITS GLORY

Whatever's the matter with Mary Jane
It cannot be that time again.
'I'm sorry Mum, I cannot "go"
The bucket soon will overflow.'
'Well never mind, I'm almost sure,
Your Dad's tomatoes need manure.
Go back outside and with all haste,
Get down the garden with that waste.'

To a younger generation who have never experienced the rigours of the privy, there must be certain questions waiting to be asked. The time has come to face them squarely, for to shirk and turn away would leave a story only half told. So what actually happened to the deposits left in the old privy, how were things kept clean and decent? Where did it all go and how? What about the smell?

Rule 1: when emptying your own privy always check which way the wind is blowing, never towards the house.

Rule 2: use the appropriate implement, a metal bowl on the end of a 9 ft wooden handle, known as a shit ladle or 'jut'.

Mr S. Waters of Southborough remembers his early days at Kilndown. 'As a child in the 1930s there were a pair of privies out the back for the two cottages. We called our privy 'the Dike' and it consisted of a wooden seat with a hole and a

61

The pair of privies at Kilndown recalled by Mr Waters. Now beautifully restored by the present owners to make a fine summerhouse.

wooden front over a pit with lime added as needed, or if you remembered! There were grub like things, grey and round, about the size of a baked bean with a tail, hanging and laying around the inside of the toilet. The back wall of the privy was supported on timber so you could dig out from the back.

'In the late 1930s the privies were updated to a bucket type. The pit was filled in, concreted over and a two-handled bucket installed and the wooden front made detachable, held in place with wooden turn buttons. This was thought to be a great advance.

'There were two buckets for the two cottages and as my father was the only man there, it was his lot to empty them. This entailed climbing over the fence into the neighbour's field, digging a hole, emptying the contents and covering over. You had to make sure of leaving a marker, like some twigs.

'To cut down on the amount of liquid in the bucket, my father erected a screen at the side of the privy, made of two pieces of corrugated iron. This cubicle had no roof and the males of the family went there to spend a penny, aiming at a piece of half round gutter so that the urine would drain away into the field.'

This exquisite area of Kent may not always have been so fragrant for Mr Waters goes on, 'I remember the Globe and Rainbow pub's waste flowed under the road into a large open ditch in the wood and many a boy has fallen into this ditch. Later on I worked at Scotney Castle timber yard where we had a wooden hut set over a drainage ditch which was mostly dry and only got flushed out when it rained. Where it went to I never knew.'

When a household's privy had a trough underneath, this had to be emptied into a hole in the vegetable garden every few months with a saucepan tied onto the end of a long pole. This was done on a Saturday night in the dark and could take four

Formerly seven privies behind 19th-century farmworkers' cottages at Sole Street, near Crundale. Originally a 'dip' or trough under the seat flowed back into a ditch.

or five hours, during which time you chain smoked! Mum stayed up and made tea and toast to keep you going and you deserved your 'lie in' next morning.

You needed to be vigilant as to where you emptied. Gerald Crouchman of Willingdon recalls a childhood at Colkins, near Faversham. 'As a family we had a dunnikin up the garden which was a bucket job and unless you kept a rota of your "burials" you'd come across sheets of *Daily Herald*, not fully decomposed. My father cursed cold weather when the ground was frozen as it meant a pickaxe job.'

Mr R. Waters of Aldington has further vivid memories. 'In the summer the buckets used to be full of maggots and the smell was awful. They were emptied in the kitchen garden at weekends, in rotation so you didn't dig in the same place twice. The soil was black after years of emptying the buckets and you could grow anything as the soil was so good.'

So in many areas you were left to your own devices and inventiveness knew no bounds when it came to sewage disposal. Waste water from the kitchen was ideal for flushing, especially if you did a lot of washing. In slop closets a simple pipe from the kitchen into a tipper suspended under the closet meant that, when full, it would automatically tip up and flush the contents into the drain. It could give you a nasty turn if you were sitting out there at the time to hear this clattering going on underneath you!

It was always easier if there was a handy stream to help waste matter on its way. Mr Moon of East Farleigh explained to me the arrangements at Hollingbourne before main drainage. 'You connected a waste pipe to the kitchen sink and the pipe would go down the garden and into the cavity under the privy thus flushing it out. Also a ditch would be dug catching the rainwater and this too would flow into the row of privies at the bottom of the garden. From there it would run into the brick drain under the

A single-seater near Frittenden built alongside a mill stream, now dried up. Behind the privy was a pit 1 yard square with a 4 inch slab cover - the contents could easily be disposed of when the stream was in full flood. Note the air vents cut into the top of the door.

street where the water from the road would join and take it on further until it ended up in the stream at Eyhorne Street.' Quite a journey!

Indeed, a lady who has lived at the Tovil end of the Loose Valley since 1948 confirmed that up to two years ago her arrangements involved a pipe to the pond across the road.

It was a wise person who stopped and considered before taking a refreshing drink from a pond or stream. Enjoying a delightful country walk on a hot summer's day, those crystal clear waters might look tempting but there was always someone in the next village who had built their privy either over or just beside that stream!

You were extremely fortunate if the disposal of your waste matter was in the hands of another. The unsung heroes of sewage must have been the night cart men with their pipes,

The jewel in the crown! The northern reredorter of St John's Hospital in Canterbury, which was founded in 1085 by Archbishop Lanfranc. It remained in use until 1948, making it the longest continuously used privy in Britain!

Originally there was probably a bench with holes on which the inmates sat. The large cavity below was flushed out by the Stour and emptied through arches into channels that led to the river. So, as Dr N. Clark of Canterbury pointed out, 'it could very reasonably be described as a "flush" toilet - twice a day at high tide!'

pumps and long-handled spades, or maybe they just carried the bucket on their shoulders and tipped it into the cart, fondly called the honeycart or lavender lorry. It was always a relief to see these gentlemen and indeed their work was acknowledged at many a council meeting. At the turn of the century the Parish Council of Cranbrook asked for the 'returns' of the 'soil cart' for the last three years to be produced. What was the Council expecting to receive?

An 80 year old lady from Chatham remembers that back in the 1920s the night cart came round late at night to empty the cesspit at the bottom of the garden. 'It was an exciting event for us and we children tried to keep awake and peep through the curtains. The cart was drawn by a horse and looked so pretty with lights all round it.'

Mrs Bryan of Chatham always 'left a bottle of beer out for the night cart men. When the cart was full it was taken to the outskirts of town and dumped; it was an area known as "the Pickle". A well-known supermarket is built on the site now!'

Tony Ruff of Willesborough lived as a child at Kempes Corner, near Boughton Aluph. 'It was a very old house with an outside toilet built onto the house as a lean-to ... a magnificent "two-seater". It was made of wood and was very draughty in the winter, as, at the rear, was a flap which could open to allow the buckets to be removed. This operation was carried out at intervals by two men who would arrive on a horse-drawn tank with an open top. The smell was appalling, especially on a hot day. You can probably guess what this vehicle was called but my mother referred to it as the "soil cart". We children were not so polite.'

According to Mr Welland of Minster, there was no time for niceties in the old part of Sheerness. Blue Town had back alleys and the bucket privies had rear flaps opening onto the alleys. Men with wheelbarrows emptied them from the alley and, to allow anyone in the privy to escape, they called, 'Shit cart's coming!'

Mr Welland, a local historian, told me how one of these carts played a heroic part in a shameful chapter of British history.

Richard Parker, an intelligent, well respected sailor, acted as spokesman, trying to better the lot of his fellow seamen. For his pains, he was hanged from the yardarm on board ship because of his part in the Nore Mutiny in 1797. His body was brought ashore by boat and was buried next to the naval dockyard at Sheerness. Feelings were running pretty high among local people at this cruel act and his distraught wife was determined to give him a Christian burial. At night, under cover of darkness and with the help of others, she dug him up and got the body away, hidden in the 'filth cart' to Gravesend. From there he was taken by boat up to London and eventually given a proper burial in a church in Whitechapel.

Another story involving a cart came from Mr Crook, who besides being a mine of information on lavatory paper knew a thing or two about buckets.

'In the 1930s we had a holiday bungalow at Seasalter. It was right on the beach with no main drainage and the Elsan toilet was built onto the corner with access from outside. It was emptied in the early hours of the morning, by a council worker pulling a large tank on iron wheels. We always reckoned anyone doing that job had to have their nose bent permanently to one side to avoid the smell.

'Dan the sanitary man came every other day and he would weave in and out of the holiday cottages with his little tank. If you wanted the Elsan emptied, you put a card with a big letter E in the window. The toilet door was never locked.

'Before the family holiday, Pop and I would go down there to see everything was all right. Well, when we opened the toilet door Pop heaved his heart up, what a sight, mess everywhere. Pop said, "That blessed bucket must be leaking. The tide's out, we'll bury it out at sea. Then we'll buy a new one in Whitstable."

'We cleaned everything up, slipped the new galvanised bucket in place and sweetened the whole thing with Elsanol, a cross between Jeyes Fluid and creosote.

'The first day of the holiday and we went to inspect the place and lo and behold the floor was flooded again. Pop was heart-broken. "Someone has pinched our bucket!"

'Pop had an idea. The next morning he got up at 4 am and hid, watching for Dan. He was horrified as Dan walked to our toilet carrying an empty, rusty old bucket. He left this in the toilet and took our full one. This was Dan's short cut, for instead of going from his cart to toilet, back to cart to empty, then returning with our bucket and finally back to the cart, he had halved his journeys. We were getting next door's old mucky leaking bucket.

'Pop was furious but what could he say? He could not complain or Dan would have told him to do it himself. So he remained tight lipped and eventually with Dan's rota system we got a decent bucket again.'

It was important that you had a good relationship with your night cart man. Mrs Carol Cooke of Marshborough relates a story told to her by Mrs Knight who had lived there as a child. 'The bucket man came round every Friday to empty the bucket which was kept on the back porch. Of course Daddy had to

A privy found in the Alkham valley, near Dover, still with its generous-sized bucket. The owner recalled, 'my father dug a trench across the garden and then emptied the contents and covered as he went along, so manuring the garden. In about 1958 things became more civilized and the local council came round every Monday morning and emptied the buckets into a lorry.' Photograph kindly supplied by Mr J.G. Harman of the Dover History Society.

A privy at Parsonage Farm, Elham; now given over to the storage of wooden fence posts.

empty the bucket into a hole every Wednesday because we were such a large family and we didn't want the bucket man to know how dirty we were.'

So, once collected, what happened then? Charles Boulding of Maidstone knew exactly. 'I went to live in Sissinghurst in 1930. The Cranbrook Rural District Council used buckets on long poles to bale out the privy midden. We used to put lime and water on to damp down the smell. It formed a skin and this repelled the flies. Later on a horse-drawn cart pulled a tank with a hand operated pump which two men would work, taking up to two hours to clear a pit 4 feet wide, 4 feet deep and 12 feet long. This pit was for the two privies, which served the six cottages with probably 25 to 30 people living there.

'Once the tank was full the cart would go to a sloping field out-side the village. The field had a 1 in 10 slope and an earth "bund" was built in a crescent shape with the open ends pointing up the hill. They opened the bottom of the tank and the muck would flow down the slope. The sun dried it and after a while the farmers brought horse-drawn dung carts and dug out the slurry and took it to put on the hop gardens, which gave you the most beautiful beer.'

Here in the Garden of England, our beer, soft fruit and vege-tables owed a lot to the quality of the waste deposits of the people of Kent. People saw it as normal to increase the fertility of their garden soil by the contents of the privy bucket. A sprinkling of earth over the deposits in the bucket or pit meant that the bac-teria in the soil gradually decomposed the waste and made excel-lent manure.

One elderly vegetarian from Frinsted, operating a bucket-and-chuckit arrangement in the local woods, roundly declared that anything passing through her must be fit for the compost heap. Scientific research in the 19th century encouraged people to waste nothing for 'the annual urine of two men contains suffi-

The present owner of Parsonage Farm, Mr John Palmer, emptying the privy bucket - of crisp packets, these days. Mr Palmer tells of showing a party of French farmers round the farm, which is a Rural Heritage Centre open during spring and summer, and recalls the difficulty of stopping them using the privy bucket.

cient mineral food for an acre of land, and mixed with ashes will produce a fair crop of turnips.'

However, 'townies' did not always understand. Mr John Palmer told me that in his father's day the waste matter from the privies of Parsonage Farm at Elham was dug into the potato patch but it was always thought best not to mention this to guests — ignorance is bliss!

Finally, when next you go to the local garden centre to buy some liquid fertiliser, think how much more satisfying it must have been to know that you had made it yourself. Marian Sargeant of Goudhurst remembers 'as a little girl going with Dad across the field to our cesspit. With our bucket on the end of some string we would gently let it down into the cesspit, hauling it back up full of rich, thick, brown liquid. This was for our tomato plants — we always had a good crop!'

[7]

ODD FLUSHINGS

A swinging chain means a warm seat.
(*Proverb*)

With the coming of the flush, certain adjustments had to be made. Initially you might view this as a step forward, but there were problems. Piped water allowed the installation of water closets either inside the house or in the garden but the untreated sewage flowed back to the rivers from where we got our drinking water. This had the effect of making the water supply dirtier

Upper class Victorians used carbon block purifiers to treat their water. These late 19th-century stoneware vessels are water filters but are often mistaken for lavatory bowls - and you can see why. From the collection of the landlord of the Three Squirrels at Stockbury.

than when we were using earth closets!

Even the chain on the first high level water systems caused a problem. Instructions had to be written on the end of the chain to 'Pull and Let Go,' otherwise people hung onto the chain causing gallons of water to be wasted.

A lady living alone at Meopham during the Second World War had a WC at the bottom of her garden. One day there was an air raid while she was in there and a bomb dropped on her house. The noise, debris and dust were horrendous. When the fire brigade arrived they found the house flattened but the WC still standing. They wrenched open the door to find the old lady, sitting there dazed and confused. Tearfully she explained, 'All I did was pull the chain!'

Without wishing to open up a North/South debate, Alice Williams of Rainham recalls that part of her childhood was spent in Tyneside with 'appalling sanitary arrangements'. In 1924 the

A collection of early lavatory chains belonging to Mr and Mrs Brian Thompson of the Brattle Farm Museum at Staplehurst.

family returned south to Gillingham and the comforts of main drainage; the outside flush lavatory was 'unimaginable luxury. My little brother had never seen such a thing and was always getting into trouble for not flushing it.'

You could get into trouble even if you did use the flush as a member of the City of Rochester Society demonstrated with this story. 'Back in the 1950s the comedian Peter Sellers played the old Chatham Empire. He told this story, using the famous Bluebottle voice from the Goon Show. Bluebottle was in lodgings with a WC at the bottom of the garden. After using the WC, he came out of the door and found a little old man in a raincoat and flat cap, standing looking at him.

'Have you just been in there?' asked the little old man.

'Yes,' said Bluebottle.

'Have you used it?' said the little old man.

'Yes,' answered Bluebottle.

'Did you see that piece of string in there?' demanded the little old man.

'Yes.'

'Did you pull it?'

'Yes,' said Bluebottle.

'I thought so,' said the little old man, 'you've just let all my bloody pigeons out!'

So you might have the luxury of a WC but if it was outside you still had the same problem as the old earth privies — namely how to avoid going outside on a cold and frosty night. Snuggled down in a warm bed on a bitter, dark night, the china chamber pot, sometimes known as the jerry, gazunder or piss pot, was the salvation of many. As a child, I can remember my mother placing one under every bed. Mine was of delicate creamware with a garland of colourful flowers of an unknown species painted round the outside. Some chamber pots had saucy sayings inside:

An outside WC could bring its own problems in cold weather. Preventing the water pipes and cistern from freezing over was a priority, as this elaborate sacking arrangement proves. A heavy brocade curtain was draped over the wooden door as well, to keep out the icy blasts.

A discarded chamber pot outside a well hidden brick-built privy in the back garden of what used to be known as Honeymoon Cottages in East Malling. Built in 1886 by the owner of the local estate, these four cottages were for deserving young couples as they started married life.

Closet chairs from the catalogue and price list of Thomas Crapper & Co dated February 1935.

Use me well, and keep me clean,
And I'll not tell what I have seen.

That was not the sort of thing to be found in our house but we were not as refined as one lady I heard about. She ran a comfortable boarding house on the south coast and because the privy was outside provided all her 'gentlemen' with chamber pots under the bed. There was one proviso; once used, the chamber pot must be placed in the corner of the bedroom with a cloth over the pot. This was so that the steam from the urine did not rise up and rust the metal springs of the bed!

80

I am often asked how ladies 'managed' in olden times. From the 18th century many carried with them the female urinal known as a 'bourdalou', made of delicate porcelain and decorated with flowers, birds or foliage. This immensely useful item, which was still in use in the 19th century, can best be described as resembling our present day gravy boat. Indeed, I was told the story by Barbara Marchant of Strood of an American antique enthusiast who, not familiar with their original use, would proudly invite his dinner guests to use his magnificent collection of 'gravy boats'.

If you disliked the idea of the chamber pot peeking out from under the bed you could always disguise it by placing the offending receptacle in a fine piece of furniture. Stools, chairs and the steps into the high feather bed could hide the pot. Even these articles are finding their way across the Atlantic. I was told recently of one being snapped up by an American for use as a salad bowl at high class dinner parties!

[8]

TALES AND CHARACTERS FROM THE GARDEN OF ENGLAND

There once was a fair Maid of Kent,
Whose trips to the loo were frequent.
She said as she flushed,
'I will not be rushed,
Nor give up my seat for a gent.'

On starting to write *Kent Privies* I was unsure whether I would have enough material — I need not have worried. Appeals on BBC Radio Kent and in local newspapers resulted in a huge response. I feel very 'privy-ledged' to have received so many lovely letters and to have made a host of new friends. A common bond shared by all those whose stories you are about to read is a terrific sense of fun. I doubt in years to come that today's lavatories will yield the same rich, dark humour.

No matter what type of privy you had, be it bucket, trench, cesspit, in the town or country, one thing that you had to be sure of was — a comfortable and firm seat.

A story told me by a member of Ditton Active Retirement Association illustrates the awful possibilities when a privy seat was unsafe. 'I lived on a farm at Leeds, just outside Maidstone. We had a two-holer at the end of the garden. I can remember poor Mother, who was six months pregnant at the time, going to use the privy. Suddenly we heard this almighty scream; the seat had collapsed under her. Mind you she had the presence of mind to grab the door handle, so she didn't fall right in.'

So where did you go when you needed a privy seat? Why to

A very substantial box type two-holer for an adult and child, to be found in the Brattle Farm Museum.

the carpenters and joiners of Kent, of course. These skilful men could furnish you with a seat of the utmost comfort, smooth, splinter free and to suit all bottom sizes.

Mr Moon of East Farleigh told me some of the secrets of his trade. 'I was an innocent young lad of 14, when I was apprenticed as a carpenter and joiner to the local coach builder in Hollingbourne in the 1920s. Hanging on the yard wall was a privy seat; the master from which all measurements were taken! Early on my old guv'nor took me to one side to explain certain "anatomical" facts of life he thought I should know. To make a good privy seat I needed to understand the shape of ladies' bottoms. According to him, the shape changed as she progressed from young, to married, to having children. For this you needed an oval shaped hole, otherwise there was a mess down the front of the box. My guv'nor's theory was that it was all to do with the way the water left the body — he was a great thinker.

83

The author examining the remains of a two-holer seat found in a woodpile in Biddenden. It has seen better days but it has been well scrubbed. Dr Johnson would have approved, for when he was told by Boswell of a privy with a padded seat, he thundered 'No Sir, there is nothing so good as the plain board.'

'When he was called to a house he was good at assessing the potential stress the privy seat would have to withstand. If the householder was a bit on the plump side he would whisper out of the corner of his mouth, "Make it a bit bigger, lad".

'The privy seats were all made by hand. When you joint a seat there is a method in joining, with a tongue between the two boards. You must get it right otherwise the joint "gives" when you sit down and you get a nasty nip where you least expect it.

'Mostly the seats were made of deal or American whitewood, especially if you wanted a wide board with few knots. You never used elm as it absorbs moisture and smells when it gets wet. Posh people would have mahogany or walnut. I never made a three-holer but I can remember a four-holer at Turkey Mill on the Ashford Road, near Maidstone.

'My guv'nor was a busy man as he was also a lay preacher and undertaker. You could say he took care of the important things of life — and death!'

Another carpenter, the aptly named Mr Wood, remembered keeping busy maintaining and making 'dozens of Thunderboxes' for the farm cottages in the Newington area. He put me in touch with Mr Daddson, a member of a well-known Newington family of carpenters, who recalled: 'In 1937 I was apprenticed to J. Brittenden and Son where my Dad was the foreman. I can remember Bob Pope delivering a privy seat we had made. He put it over his head and it sat on his shoulders like a horse collar and off he pedalled on his bike with his head peering through, all the way from Newington to Sittingbourne.

'Another time we were installing a new privy seat for a right finicky woman who kept trying it and saying it wasn't level. Well I knew it was but she wasn't having any of it. So I had to build up one side of the privy seat until she thought it level. I didn't like to tell her that it was her that was not right. I reckon one side of her bottom was fatter than the other!'

85

The pretty village of Loose, near Maidstone. It can be pronounced as 'loose' as in 'loose change' or 'looze' as in the plural of 'loo'! And yes, the locals are fed up with the jokes.

Former carpenter and joiner Mr Charles Boulding of Maidstone could give me the exact measurements needed for the oval hole in the seat: 9 inches wide and 11 inches long. He recounted for me the following story. 'In 1944 a doodlebug struck Hawkhurst Moor church, causing extensive damage. In 1949 the rebuilding of the church began.

'The mason in charge of the work was about 70 years old and very portly. He had a mate, a stout Irishman, and the pair of them stayed in a local pub called the Cricketers while the work was being done. Every evening they spent in the pub drinking as much beer as they could swallow. They would then retire to their bedroom in the pub attic, taking a bucket with them. This bedroom had a dormer window onto a tiled roof at the back of the pub. Needing to "go" in the night was a simple affair; into the bucket. When the bucket was full they would open the window and empty it onto the tiles, without a thought as to where it went.

'One morning the old mason came down extra early. By the back door of the pub was a 40 gallon waterbutt full of water from the roof, and the landlady was filling her kettle. The old mason said, "Do you always use that water?" "Yes," she replied. "'Tis the finest water in all Kent and I'm just making you your breakfast cup o' tea." He never drank another cup in that pub.

'While rebuilding there had to be a privy on site; a tin hut with a pit at the back. Whenever the mason used the privy, the young fellows working there threw stones at the tin, making a devil of a noise but he could never catch them.

'One day the young man, who the mason reckoned was the ringleader, had to use it and the mason, creeping up behind the privy, lifted half a gravestone high above his head and hurled it into the back of the pit. The resulting splash caused the privy contents to cover the young man. It was so bad he had to be hosed down.'

You had to be able to take a joke if you worked on a building site, as this story from Mr H. Ottaway of Faversham proves. 'In the 30s there were no portaloos and building site privies consisted of a corrugated iron shed, erected over a hole dug in the ground. There was no seat but a plank of 4 x 2 wood fixed across the shed. Stroud and Roberts, builders of Whitstable, were constructing houses on a site and young "Cocky Roberts", son of the boss, was an apprentice carpenter at the time. He was also a practical joker and with his carpenter's saw sabotaged the privy seat by sawing halfway through it. Of course, the first unfortunate labourer to answer a call of nature, upon placing his weight on the plank, immediately broke it and he was dropped into the hole to be covered by all its contents. "Cocky" beat a hasty retreat. I don't know if he was ever caught but he went on to become the boss!'

Making a bit of a splash seems to have been a childhood preoccupation of Reg Bunn of Chatham, who as a lad living at Wouldham would throw penny 'bangers' into the privy bucket to see the effect or the 'flash in the pan'!

Reg goes on, 'Our privy was at the top of the garden and backed onto our neighbours'. It consisted of a board with a hole, across two brick pillars, a board at the front and a galvanised bucket. It was like this up to 1960 and I can remember digging a path through 5 feet of snow and sitting on that board trying to keep my coat on in sub zero temperatures. It was there I had my first smoke "roll up" of Dad's Golden Virginia and later on I would stand guard late at night when my girl-friend Carole used it — she came from the town so was used to an indoor flush.'

Carole went on to marry Reg but the problem of 'courting' a loved one with a primitive privy when you were used to town flushing is neatly told by Stan of Staplehurst. 'My story took place in the late 40s. I originated from Chatham where we had a flush toilet and I started courting a young lady from Staplehurst. My young lady lived in a farm cottage with a bucket type privy down the bottom end of a very long garden. Her married sister and husband and small family lived quite close, also in a farm cottage.

'One Sunday my young lady and her family were all invited to the married sister's for Sunday tea. It was winter time and after tea in the evening I needed to use the "loo".

'Their privy was situated in a large shed across a yard. It was very dark and I had no light at all but I had used the privy a couple of times before so I groped about a little until I found it. I sat down and to my surprise I did not hear anything drop but felt myself touching something. I wiped myself using all the squares of newspaper which were hanging on a piece of string by the corner.

'I went back into the cottage and said to my young lady's brother-in-law, "Jim, I think your loo wants emptying." Jim replied, "It can't do, I only emptied it this morning, I'll go and have a look." Jim came back and said, "You didn't lift off the board covering the bucket!" You can imagine what I had done. I felt like crawling under the table! Incidentally, I have been married to my young lady for 45 years, so she did not hold it against me.'

I was told of a similar incident by a member of Maidstone Active Retirement Association. 'The coal shed and privy were side by side in the yard. The owners wanted a modern toilet put in and when the plumber called he advised that the cistern would be better installed where the coal was kept and so to put the lavatory in the coal hole and the coal in the lavatory. No one told me. Visiting one dark evening and desperate to go, I did a pee on the coal.'

Not everyone was anxious to rush headlong into 'modernising'. David Kemp's grandfather resolutely stood out against the forces of flushing. 'We had an outside bucket privy at Park Court Farm at Birchington, where we were tenants for 76 years. It was Grandma's dearest wish to have a flush, indoor lavatory and Grandfather was eventually persuaded to go and see the owners of the farm, the Powell-Cotton family. They agreed he could install a modern lavatory but he would have to pay. "How much is it going to cost?" demanded Grandfather. On being told the figure he was appalled and declared roundly, "I've shit into that bucket all my life and I'll go on shitting for a bit longer!" True to his word, that outside privy bucket was still there right up until he retired in 1962.

'He was a great joker, my Grandfather. The bucket was in a tin shed at the bottom of the garden and when lady visitors used it, he liked nothing better than to throw a brick onto the tin roof. Bits of lime would flake off the roof, the noise was deafening and the occupant would rush out, scared stiff.

'One day Aunt Lou came down from London to visit. No one liked her as she was a strict old so and so. The younger members of the family knew what time train she was due on and thought they could time her arrival and her need to use the privy. They tarred the privy seat but alas my father's grandmother went instead and got tar all over her bottom. It took her husband ages to get it all off.'

Kent abounds in colourful characters. Sailor Rye was a legend in his own lifetime and I am grateful to Jim of Maidstone Active Retirement Association for putting me in touch with Sailor Rye's son, Don, who recounted just a little of his father's history.

'Born in 1879 and living to age 94, Sailor Rye described himself as "Queen Victoria's Bad Bargain", on account of his 25 years in the Navy and 54 years on a pension. Retiring from the Navy in the 1920s, he settled down to family life in Wickhambreaux. As befitted a retired Chief Petty Officer, he proceeded to organise civilian life. He and the Vicar together with the local school master "ran" the village.

'One of Sailor Rye's many roles was the Village Librarian. He used a shed next to his house in which to keep the library books. At one end of this shed was a separate little room housing the family Elsan toilet. There was an oil lamp in "the library" for dark evenings but none in the toilet. This made for difficulties for the family when using the toilet after dark, as the door between the two rooms had to be kept open. "The library" always had an unusual smell to it.

'Sailor Rye had a small market garden at the back of Wickhambreaux school. With the zeal of a born entrepreneur, he negotiated the rights to the waste matter from the school lavatories and together with the contents of the Elsan this was used on the market garden to enhance his produce. His vegetables were renowned throughout Wickhambreaux but he was perhaps best known for his astonishingly fruitful fig tree. He would sell the figs to the Vicar, thereby fulfilling his Christian duty, maintaining the inner cleanliness and regularity of the Church's representative in Wickhambreaux. Any left over were offered for sale to the villagers. Village life must have run pretty smoothly.'

There certainly is 'something about a sailor' as Marian Sargeant of Goudhurst remembers when describing her happy childhood in the early 1950s. 'Dad had a pet parrot called Laura whom he loved dearly. He had brought her home from the sea on settling down with Mum and that darned parrot loved him just as much. Dad would take Laura outside with him, open the privy door and while he shaved in the shed, she would sit on the top of this door keeping him company. Laura

Deep in the countryside around Smarden, a brick-built, two-holer affectionately known as Ivy Lodge, now completely given over to nature. Set a fair
distance from the house, it could be creepy in the winter and the door bears
the scorch marks from the tilly lamp.

had a vicious beak and would peck away at the top of the door, in fact it was so badly damaged we had to rehang it upside down.

'The privy door had a 4 inch gap at the top and swung outwards. As a little girl the toilet paper on the back of the door was always an arm and a half away and difficult to reach. If you remembered, you got hold of the end of the Bronco roll first and then climbed onto the seat with it firmly in your hands. There was a snag to this because if my little sister wanted to go, she would shout "Hurry up", swing the door open and there would be yards of Bronco everywhere.

'It was very dark in our privy which we called the Knickies. My mother had a shock one evening. You used to keep the door a little ajar to allow some light in and she was sitting there at dusk minding her own business when she became aware that she was not alone. Feeling, rather than seeing, a presence, she pushed the door closed and caught...a rat! What a shriek!'

You were rarely alone in a garden privy. It was not just human company, often very welcome, out there in the dark night but the unknown creatures. Who knew what was lurking under the seat or round the door? It was a wise person who walked to the privy with heavy footsteps and rattled the latch before entering. This gave the rats and mice notice and a sporting chance of moving on.

You could be sure of plenty of flies and bluebottles, which was why privies had a lid. Indeed, I was told of an expression used by a Westerham lady whenever she saw a baby with a little round nose, 'She has a nose like a button on a privy lid.'

More formidable were Mrs Bryan's stink bees which lived in the brickwork of her cesspit in Chatham. 'They never hurt you but they used to fly out at you sometimes and you could hear them humming below you.'

Spiders in corners, maybe, but weasels lying in wait? Here is a tale told by Mrs Ruth Smith of Gillingham which makes the blood run cold! 'Some years ago out in the country a young lady visited the earth closet on a dark evening. As she sat down on the privy seat a weasel grabbed her bottom. Unable to shake it off, she ran screaming into the house where the lodger, being the only one at home, had to prise it off.' (Author's note: Definition of a weasel — a small, nimble, ferocious, reddish-brown, **carnivorous** animal.)

Mrs Smith has known her own moment of horror when 'I went with my parents to visit relatives at Riverhead. I visited the toilet in the garden and a huge spider was stretched across the pan. I went back indoors and was laughed at for being afraid but when one of them went to see, they were shocked and killed it. As the garden was near the goods train yard I wondered if it came from foreign parts in a case?'

Sometimes you could be a bit over enthusiastic in dealing with vermin in your privy. Carol Cooke of Marshborough told of dark deeds at Sunnyside Cottages. 'Going back to the 40s, when there was a pub just down the road, Ol' Frank and his Dad were having trouble with foxes getting into the privy and making a mess. One night, when Frank returned from the pub, he heard a rustling in the privy in the dark. Determined to discourage the foxes once and for all, he got out his shotgun, pointed the barrel up through a hole in the bottom of the door … and fired. A loud scream revealed that Ol' Frank had shot his Dad in the backside. Everyone knew about it because Frank's Dad didn't sit in church for months afterwards.'

Not all experiences were awful. From Rex Lancefield's *Recollections of Rural Life Around Godmersham, Crundale and Waltham* is a memory supplied by Mr Graves of Maidstone as told to him by his Uncle Owen. 'Mum looked after the chickens and raised about a hundred a year for the farmer and got five pounds a

The privy behind the Three Squirrels at Stockbury.

year for it. We had an outside toilet with a big seat and a small seat. I got friendly with one of the hens and it used to go into the toilet, sit on the small seat and lay its egg. After a while I used to follow her in, sit on the big seat, put the hen on my lap and she laid her egg in there!'

Less welcome was the discovery made by a Sittingbourne lady's grandmother on going out to her privy in Sheerness, one dark and windy night. There was no light and the seat was a dark mahogany that stretched from wall to wall. On trying to sit down Grandmother found her descent hindered — by a large dog stretched across the mahogany seat!

Even if you used your privy without anything attacking you inside, it was not always possible to leave with any kind of dignity. A tale of another canine came from Mr John Palmer of

Hens seem to be drawn to a privy. Behind the Three Squirrels at Stockbury, near Sittingbourne, is a brick-built outhouse, filled now with garden tools. It was possible to clear a little space to find the remains of a two-holer. A hen had laid her eggs down one hole and was quite ruffled at being disturbed!

There was no lock on the privy at Parsonage Farm at Elham. The string tied on the handle was there to hold the door shut. However, to pull your trousers up you had to let go, and for a few vital seconds you were at your most vulnerable.

Elham. Lucky enough to have **two** privies, he told me this story, passed onto him by his father. 'We were a big family of 10 children. One of the daughters had recently married and she and her new husband had come on a visit. The new son-in-law had to spend a penny during the night and so crept out of the back door and down the garden path to the brick-built privy. Once ready to return to the warmth of the matrimonial bed, he found his way barred by a growling, snarling farm dog. The dog, thinking she had caught an intruder, refused to let him pass and he, too embarrassed to call for help, retreated back to the privy for safety, where he spent a cold, uncomfortable night.'

It was not only dogs that could keep you at bay. A turkey was a fearsome sight just outside the privy door. 'Old Gobbler' prevented many from performing their natural bodily functions. Even smaller birds could take hostages, as this story heard at West Malling proved. 'We lived in the middle of a wood at Keeper's Cottage, Shoreham, near Sevenoaks. It was during the Second World War and two of my sisters were working but could come home at weekends. We kept chickens and a very fierce cock bantam. This cock bantam would let my sisters go into the privy but wouldn't let them come out. If you tried and turned your back on him, he would go for the heels. My sisters would stay in the privy, with the door firmly shut and shout for father. He would come down the garden path and sort that cock bantam out just long enough for them to get back to the cottage.'

Mr Ron Terry of Sevenoaks encountered many an eccentric and had many tales from a career as a Public Health Inspector. In his time he has been threatened with the contents of a bucket closet as well as immersion in a midden. He remembered one old gentleman whose house was on a bank beside a main road. He burnt his stairs for heat and fitted a ladder instead. He then turned to his outside wooden privy and dismantled it for firewood. He was seen from time to time in the open air above the bank, seated on his, by now, seatless pan doing what he had to do!

People were often far from grateful, as Ron recalled. 'We had a persistent problem with a blocked loo at one dwelling and called for help from the Council Works department. Rods and staff arrived and we found a manhole nearby and on removing the cover saw a dryish channel. We inserted the rods and pushed hard to clear the obstruction. Loud screams were heard and an irate lady soon joined us as she had been duly enthroned at the time.'

Finally, you were not even safe from your nearest and dearest in the privy, as shown by a story told to me by a member of the Monday Club at Gillingham Adult Education Centre. 'A young man returned home to Kent after serving some time in the Army. He had been used to flush facilities in the barracks and kept nagging his old Mum and Dad to update the old garden privy.

'Dad was having none of it. "If that old privy is good enough for your mother and me, it's good enough for you." The argument raged on until one day, in desperation, the son said to his father, "I'm giving you one last chance to do something about that privy." "No," said father, "that privy stays." "Right," said the son, "In that case I'm going to do something about it." With that, he gets out a grenade he's been hiding, pulls the pin and lobs it at the privy. Well the privy came crashing down, wood, brick, everything in a heap. Father looked on horrified. "What have you done? Mother was in there!" He rushed up the garden path shouting, "Myrtle, Myrtle, are you all right? Speak to me." From the rubble came a small voice, "It's all right George, I'm OK, it must be something I've eaten!"'

A story with a happy ending (photograph kindly supplied by Sevenoaks District Council). Behind a pair of cottages near Hever, a row of three privies, seen here before renovation...

...and after some financial help from the Council - a little bit of social history preserved. The end privy is a two-holer for a mother and child, the centre a two-holer and the other one a spacious single seater.

[9]

KENT HOP PICKERS

'Kent, sir — Everybody knows Kent — apples,
cherries, hops, and women.'
(*Mr Jingle in Pickwick Papers by Charles Dickens*)

An important feature of Kent country life was hop picking. Part of history now but an interesting cultural phenomenon that saw thousands from the East End of London flocking to Kent annually. At the height of the hop picking 250,000 'strangers' came by foot, lorry or railway. The sanitary implications for such huge numbers needs to be examined and we shall not shirk from so doing.

Mr Elkins of Faversham, who has lived all his life in the town, told me, 'The arrangement for hop picking was that prior to picking, the town crier would tour the streets of the town and announce that hop picking would commence on such and such date. He would carry a bell and shout at the top of his voice.'

Hop pickers were divided into 'home' pickers and those down from London. The Londoners in the hop pickers' huts might have a simple privy in a tin hut at the end of the row, but once out in the hop field you were on your own.

Betty Millen of Tenterden remembers hop picking with relations where 'we went into the woods next to the hop garden.' Susie Filmer of Shadoxhurst has more painful memories, of 'taking a very long run to the bottom of the hop alley where all the seeded stinging nettles grew and there you stooped down and finished quick. A dock leaf was very handy and the low bines made a shelter.'

Hop fields near Yalding.

A corrugated tin single-seater privy for hop pickers at the Museum of Kent Life at Maidstone. Note the tin bath hanging on the wall of the communal cook house. Early living quarters were primitive and unsanitary and some typical hop pickers' huts can be seen at the museum.

Hop bines came in very useful, as May Gurr of Canterbury told me, together with an article of clothing few will know about. 'I am sure there were no privies in the hop fields in my young days in the 1920s, judging by the antics of the mums. They used a screen of picked bines when they were in need and what was more hilarious they never pulled their skirts up! Most of them were in possession for hop picking of a type of knicker, "two legs on tape" as they called them. So you only had to squat and make out that you were picking up dropped hops.'

Joan Jeffery of Petts Wood was one of the Londoners who came down to Kent. 'Every year my mother took us children hop picking to Three Chimneys Farm at Goudhurst. The accommodation, by the standards of the day, was excellent with brick huts, brick cookhouses and a brick privy. The privies were situated across a field and were over a trench, no bucket just a hole. There were four to six large holes plus about four smaller and lower for children, all in the one compartment. My brother tells me that the men's section was the same. No arrangements were made for when we were picking in the field, you just had to make use of a convenient hedge.'

Mrs Ellen Moss of Crundale remembered as a child hop picking before the war in the Paddock Wood and Goudhurst areas. 'Two weeks before hop picking started Mum would go down to get the hut ready. It was a corrugated tin hut and the cattle were kept in there during the winter but despite this Mum would wallpaper and put up her own curtains. Cockneys were very proud and kept their huts spotless. There were three families in all and we would hire a lorry to take us to Kent. Dad was working so came down at weekends. We never minded missing school. There was no privacy with a gap at the top of the partition with next door but what I hated most were the privies. Tin huts with three and four-holers over a pit and some with just half doors. Where we came from in Limehouse and Stepney we had flush lavatories.'

Sometimes the hop picking huts were nicely aired. Margaret Angus recalled 'living in Sevenoaks during the war and as a school girl I belonged to the Young Farmers' Club run by my grammar school. We would be sent off for the month of August to help on Kent farms and I went to Captain Beale's farm at Sissinghurst. Part of the excitement for the girls was living in the hop picking huts.

We were there the month before the hop pickers so the huts were nicely aired by the time they came. The communal privy was in one of the hoppers' huts so you had some privacy. It was a big hole, as I remember it, with a wooden seat across and plenty of Jeyes Fluid nearby for disinfecting. It was very smelly but it did not spoil our fun and we all looked upon the experience as doing our bit for the war effort.'

Ellen Moss remembers on the last day the Londoners would have a 'knees-up' and sing:

Now that hopping's over and the money is all spent.
How I wish I'd never gone, a-hopping down in Kent.

Yet, sadly, not all those who came 'a-hopping' lived to return home and I close this chapter with a sorry tale. 'My family were Kentish yeoman and lived at Boughton, near Faversham. They had a privy at the bottom of the garden, right next to a very deep well. My grandmother was obliged every hop picking to house two young men who came down from London for the hop picking.

'On Sunday evening my grandmother would make these two young men go to church in their best suits and bowler hats. One Sunday only one young man came back from church. He told grandmother that the other lad had not gone to church and it was his opinion that he was unhappy and had gone back to London.

'One month later grandmother went to get some water from the well and there, floating on the surface, was a bowler hat! The poor young man had gone to the privy before church, and in the dark he had missed the privy and fallen down the well. They got the body out with grappling hooks but it gave poor grandmother a turn, not least the fact that he had been in her drinking water!'

[1 0]

Posh Privies

> However high and mighty
> With fortune, wealth and fame,
> Once seated on the privy
> We share a common aim.

The humble cottager might grapple with the disposal of the contents of his privy bucket and the town dweller anxiously await the night cart men to clean the cesspits but there were some who could boast very flush facilities.

Consider the arrangements once available to naval officers of a certain rank when Chatham Dockyard was a flourishing naval establishment. The Commissioner's House in Chatham Historic Dockyard must boast one of the finest lavatories in all Kent. Affectionately known as the 'Blue Loo', it was extensively renovated in the 1990s by the Chatham Historic Dockyard Trust.

Ray Christopher of the *Medway News* told me of a Rear Admiral entertaining an Admiral to dinner in the Commissioner's House. A convivial evening left the Admiral 'a few sheets to the wind'. Asking to use the 'Blue Loo', he left the table, but after some time failed to return. A search party sent out found the Admiral sitting on the 'loo', transfixed by the tiles, trying to count them and find a pair that matched.

Also in Chatham Historic Dockyard is the beautifully restored paddle steamer *Kingswear Castle*. The loo on board really is a 'throne' as you must mount two steps to be seated. Captain John Megoran explained to me that there had to be sufficient height above the waterline to get a good flush.

The 'Blue Loo' lined with Delft-style tiles made in Lambeth in 1710, each handpainted with scenes from pastoral life.

You cannot move far in Kent without coming across Mr Charles Dickens. He lived, slept, visited and wrote his way round the county. The Poor Travellers' House in Rochester High Street, for example, was honoured with a visit from Mr Dickens in 1854. The plaque commemorating this historic occasion is fixed to the outside of the privy, tucked away in a corner of the exquisite garden at the rear.

I am very grateful to the Mayor of the City of Rochester upon Medway for allowing me to photograph the lavatory in the Mayor's Parlour at the old Town Hall in Chatham.

A more difficult proposition was getting inside the Castle Club of Rochester. This 'gentlemen only' dining club has strict rules on not admitting females. Rumour had it that within these manly portals lurked an original Thomas Crapper. Having telephoned to ask the help of a friend, David Tester of Rochester, I later discovered our conversation written up in their newsletter.

The water for flushing on the *Kingswear Castle* is provided by a steam pump. The experience can be sampled on one of the regular cruises on the river Medway and the Thames.

It is not known whether Dickens was ever seated within. Owned by the Richard Watts' Charity, the house and tiny garden are open to the public. Sadly, the privy no longer performs its original function.

This handsome loo exudes the gravitas befitting an item of furniture fit for a mayor. No jokes here about the mayoral chain!

The author rejected the suggestion that she should dress up as a man, but in the end she got her photograph of 'the throne' at the Castle Club - husbands have their uses!

'I received an amazing telephone call the other day. A female voice said, "Do you have a Thomas Crapper at the club?" Now, I know most of the members but one Thomas Crapper was new to me, neither could I remember that quite outstanding name coming up for membership. I therefore replied that I didn't know a Thomas Crapper and that we definitely did not have a member of that name.

'The voice said, "No, you don't understand, the loo upstairs, by the billiard room, is it a Thomas Crapper?" Well now, this female, how did she even know that we had a loo on the first floor, and how dare she refer to our superb throne as anything other than "the Thunderbox". Ladies, I am glad to say, are not allowed into the club and the Thunderbox, as far as is known, has existed without ever having experienced the dubious privilege of cosseting a lady's bottom, or using its powerful flush in

111

assisting the removal of female deposits!

'The item after checking was indeed verified as a Thomas Crapper, the Rolls Royce of loos. Now just remember that when next you require the abbreviation of his name and sit, majestically, in one of the best Gentlemen's Clubs in existence, on one of the best water closets in existence.'

[11]

PRIVATE WOES IN PUBLIC PLACES

I do not like this place at all,
The seat is too high and the hole is too small.

You lay yourself open to the obvious retort
Your bottom's too big and your legs are too short.

Whatever your arrangement at home there, comes a time when you are forced upon the mercies of a public privy.

The Frittenden Historical Society supplied me with an extract from a Parish Vestry Meeting held in the early part of the 19th century. They met 'to consider the **necessity** or **propriety** of moving the Public Privy from its present position having completely spoilt the water in the well of Edward Murphy.' Whatever they decided, we would do well to note that there is no public lavatory in Frittenden now!

Lavatories are not often found in old churches, as Mary Lawrence of Hildenborough Afternoon WI recalls. 'Airing my grievances to a visiting Bishop over the lack of a "convenience" at my little rural church, I expressed a wish that at my demise a suitable structure should be situated within the church grounds to provide "instant relief" for all who visit this church. The Bishop replied with a wry smile, "I will see to it personally that your wishes are acceded to: dedicated and suitably named — 'The Mary Loo'."'

Using communal lavatories at work could be hazardous. Mr Harfleet of Medway was an apprentice shipwright in Chatham Dockyard before the Second World War. 'Our lavatories were

A friend (with torch) investigates the substantial flint-built privy in the churchyard behind Selling church. The women and children would have been well served by this two-holer during a long sermon - gentlemen had to make other arrangements.

114

Approached via an open, walled, spiral passage, the recently renovated adult
and child two-holer at Selling.

in two rows facing each other but with a partition wall down the
middle. None of them had doors, so that the Supervisor could
walk up and down, making sure no one was malingering.
Underneath was a communal trough which was flushed automatically from a tank. We apprentices would get newspapers or
oily cotton waste, set light to them and launch the burning
bundle down the trough underneath the seats. With a bit of
luck you could singe at least five bums!'

Of course the Dockyard at that time was full of naval person-
nel who needed lavatories by rank. Mr Harfleet explained that
in the same privy block, a few feet apart, was a row of doors
labelled: Ratings Only, POs Only, CPOs Only, Warrant Officers Only, Officers Only. Going to the lavatory was no leveller
in this establishment.

Mrs Winnie Rolfe, now of St Albans, wrote of working in the
Wages Department in the Dockyard in 1946. 'We were at the

The chute from the officers' two-holer at Fort Amherst, built between 1756 and the mid 1800s and one of the best preserved Napoleonic forts in the country. There was no outlet so the steps were for some poor soldier to go down and clear it out with a bucket and shovel. The shaft at the side was possibly to give some air but would have relieved the build-up of methane gas.

116

A gentlemen's Victorian lavatory resembling a sentry box, complete with Grenadier Guard, at the Black Lion at Lynsted.

117

top of a three storey building. To one side of this building and below us was a Dockyard toilet, with no roof to it, just a light glass cover. The ladies of the Wages Department soon caused a roof to be provided: it must have been the fastest piece of building work done in the Dockyard for many a day.'

People working on the land were not so fortunate. Mrs Jenny Wells of Canterbury went fruit picking and was shocked to find no facilities. 'I complained, they said no one had complained before, but I was lucky and they put up some portaloo type toilets, not as good as they are now, but adequate.'

Few facilities were provided and those described by Mr R. Waters seem fairly typical. 'When the farm at Courtap Street had seasonal workers for picking potatoes, sugar beet, wurzel or broad beans we had a big hole dug in the field. Planks were laid over the top and a wooden box with a hole was stood on top of the planks, with sailcloth round the outside. The smell was really awful, plus all those maggots underneath you.'

This may sound familiar to all ex Girl Guides and Boy Scouts who have memories of childhood camps and the 'lats' on the edge of the field. Mr Harfleet was a Boy Scout in 1938. 'You would dig a trench and put some canvas round for privacy, then secure a peg in the ground with some rope round it. The other end of the rope was tied to a piece of round wood about 12 inches long. This was the KYBO stick you held onto as you squatted over the trench and it stopped you falling in. Keep Your Bowels Open!'

In the Second World War the Land Army girls from the town often found rural life primitive. Mrs Susie Filmer of Shadoxhurst picked apples during her Land Army days. 'A bombing raid came on quickly and we rushed for shelter under the wagon. When it was all over, we emerged to see a crater with a large apple tree in it. The tree grew up to land level, so the hole, covered with the branches, became our private place to spend a

The Black Boy at Halling is so old that the building is mentioned in the Domesday Book. It can also boast a Victorian trough in the men's loo. The landlady, Christina Kay, encourages her gentlemen customers to drop coins there. Every month she puts on her trusty 'marigolds' and fishes the money out - after a good wash it is sent off to a local charity.

119

High in the woods above a house in lovely Crundale, a brick-built two-holer, known in that area as a 'tivvy'. The snow on the steps is a reminder of how cold it must have been to use it, although the magnificent view across the Crundale valley from the seat must have been some compensation.

penny.

'Later the farm wagon brought a wooden loo, like a sentry box, painted green and brown and no roof. It was dug into the hedgerow but it rocked about in the winter winds. Up near the farm the German POWs built their privy of straw bales with a thatch roof and a notice in blue " 'HERREN".'

Susie remembers earlier days at school. 'Our school was out in the country at Charing Heath. Teacher's bike was kept in the Infants' privy. There were eight very small cubicles with half swing doors, and under each low seat was a small bucket. The elder girls had to take turns to see all was well, buttoning up the young ones' flaps. After school an old man was waiting with his hand cart to take all the tin buckets away to empty onto the heath amongst the heather and yellow gorse.'

AND FINALLY... To young people reading this book, I am sure you have shuddered at some of the stories, the smells and sights recalled within these pages. Yet consider how predictable everything is now and how squeamish we have become. Where is the adventure? To those for whom this book has brought memories flooding back, you needed stamina and courage to use a privy. It has made you the people you are today. Our present hygienic lavatory in tasteful colours is all very well, but will it be able to provide the tales of the future? Will there be a book in 50 years time on the Kent privies of the 1990s? I think not.

Found near Hever.

A Privy by any Other Name

A 'certain' place
Asterroom
Aunt Jane's
Biffy
Bog
Boghouse
Bombay
Chamber of commerce
Chamberlain pianos ('bucket
   lav')
Chuggie
Closet
Cludgie
Comfort station
Crapper box
Crapphouse
Crapping castle
Crapping kennel
Dike
Dinkum-dunnies
Doneks
Dover House
Dubs
Dubby
Duffs
Dunnakin

Dunnekin
Dunnikin
Dunnick
Dyke
Garden loo
Garderobe
Go and have a Jimmy Riddle
Go and have a Tim Tit
Going to pick daisies
Going to see a man
   about a dog
Going to stack the tools
Going to the George
Going to the groves
Gone where the wind is
   always blowing
Gong
Gong house
Heads
Here is are
Holy of holies
Home of rest
Honk
House of commons
House of office
Houses of parliament

Jakes	The boggy at the bottom
Jerry-come-tumble	The bush
Jericho	The dispensary
Karzi	The dunny
Klondike	The grot
Knickies	The halting station Hoojy-boo (attributed to Dame Edith Evans)
Larties	
Latrine	
Lav	The house where the emperor goes on foot
Lavatory	
Little house	The hum
Loo	The jakers
My aunts	The jampot
Nessy	The japping
Netty	The John
Out the back	The lats
Petty	The long drop
Place of easement	The opportunity
Place of repose	The ping-pong house
Place of retirement	The proverbial
Reading room	The Sammy
Round-the-back	The shants
Shit-hole	The shot-tower
Shittush	The sociable
Shooting gallery	The tandem (a two-holer)
Shunkie	The thinking house
Slash house	The throne room
The backhouse	The watteries

The wee house

The whajucallit

Three and more seaters

Thunder box

Tivvy

Two seaters

Widdlehouse

Windsor Castle

'Yer Tiz'

The penny house

The plumbing

The porcelain pony

The water box

Umtag (Russian version of the WC)

Going to inspect the plumbing

The urinal

Waterloo

Especially for WCs:

Adam & Eve

Chain of events

Flushes and blushes

The term 'privy' is an Early Middle English word which derives from the Latin 'privatus' meaning apart or secret.

ACKNOWLEDGEMENTS

I would like to express my grateful thanks to all the people who so kindly let me photograph their privies and who took the time to write and telephone with their stories and memories.

In my efforts to find the privies of Kent my thanks must also go to the following:

BBC Radio Kent
Medway News
Kent Today
Bygone Kent
Kentish Express
Kentish Gazette
Faversham Times
Sevenoaks Chronicle
Kent — Magazine of the County Society

Ron Terry
Barbara Marchant
Sarah Pearson of Charing & District Local History Society
The Reverend Canon Ingram Hill
Brigid Longley of the Cranbrook Museum

The Museum of Kent Life at Maidstone
Canterbury Archaeological Trust Ltd
Dartford Borough Museum for the 'Great Dartford Privy Hunt'
The staff of Sittingbourne Library and the County Library

Rochester upon Medway City Council
Sevenoaks District Council
Tunbridge Wells Borough Council

The WIs of East and West Kent, especially the Farleighs

All the Kent Local History Societies, who were so enthusiastic

My husband Ray, who thought he had retired but found himself my research assistant.